ARWYN HERMAN

MAKE COLLEGE COUNT

**The Ultimate Guide to College Life, Learn Valuable Information and
Tips on How You Can Prepare for an Exciting Journey of College Life**

Descrierea CIP a Bibliotecii Naţionale a României
ARWYN HERMAN
    MAKE COLLEGE COUNT. The Ultimate Guide to College
Life, Learn Valuable Information and Tips on How You Can
Prepare for an Exciting Journey of College Life / Arwyn
Herman – Bucharest: Editura My Ebook, 2020
    ISBN

ARWYN HERMAN

MAKE COLLEGE COUNT

The Ultimate Guide to College Life, Learn Valuable Information and Tips on How You Can Prepare for an Exciting Journey of College Life

My Ebook Publishing House
Bucharest, 2020

TABLE OF CONTENTS

FOREWORD

College life is one of the most crucial parts of education. It is an educational chapter in your life that would effectively and completely enhanced your skills towards achieving your goals in life. It serves as a stepping stone for every people in reaching their goals.

Although it might be one of the most difficult chapters in your life in terms of education, these chapters still helps in arousing your maturity in thinking and dealing with other people and coping with the different problems in your life. All the things that you may be learning during this chapter can either be good or bad but they may help you in becoming a holistically developed person with the right value and attitude towards life.

For people who want to get to know more about college life, reading this ebook would clearly explain to you several and essential facts about college education and the things you need to prepare for.

Ready -> Get Set -> Go College!

Prepare Yourself for an Exciting Journey of College Life

CHAPTER 1

BASIC PREPARATION FOR COLLEGE

Synopsis

College life is considered to be a harsh chapter of life since there are several changes that you might be experiencing in this particular stage. Preparing to enter for college is a difficult task particularly if you don't have any idea as to how you are going to deal with this fast approaching chapter of your school life. There are several things that you need to prepare in order to have an assurance that entering college would not be as difficult and harsh as what other people are saying.

Taking your first step in college would always make way for confusion and nervousness to arise. Hence, in order to help every student in order to deal with this feeling, there are several tips they should always consider in order to effectively and conveniently prepare for college without thinking too much worries. Following some of these tips could be very essential towards a well-prepared self in college.

Basic Preparation Tips for College

Course to Take

Student need to make sure that before graduating in high school, they should be already familiar with the course they wanted to pursue in college. Make sure that the course you are going to take would be based on your interest, skills and abilities. This is because students who pursue the course they really wanted would be very successful in return.

School to Enroll

After deciding on what course to take the next thing you should prepare is more on choosing the best school that could inculcate right knowledge, values, skills and attitudes that would mold you as a person and will definitely develop your skills in your chosen course.

School Requirements

You need to prepare for all the school materials that are highly needed in your chosen course. Apart from paper, pen, notebooks and all other basic school supplies you need to prepare for some of the required school requirement that the school would be requiring you to submit. As early as possible make sure to be familiar with all the basic school supplies that is highly needed in your chosen course.

Interviews and Exams

Preparing for college would be very difficult since there are interviews and exams provided by different college institutions as part of their admission test. This is just to test if you are capable to enroll in your chosen course.

This is also one way of assessing skills, knowledge and aptitude of the students before allowing them to enter college. Hence as a responsible student who wanted to make themselves completely prepared to enter college, they must always study in order to pass college exams and interviews.

Scholarship Programs

Once you are preparing for college, get familiar with some of the scholarship programs offered in the specified school you wanted to enroll. Getting to know some of this scholarship program is very essential since it could greatly help you and your parents to lessen college expenses. Being a scholar of any type of scholarship program would always arouse your interest and would motivate you all the time to strive more effort and time in studying.

CHAPTER 2

GREAT STRATEGIES TO SCORE FLYING COLORS IN SAT & ACT

Synopsis

One of the most common exams that aim to assess the all the learnings of the students in their school as well as in all other basic areas is the SAT and the ACT. Scholastic Aptitude Test is a test that assesses student's critical reasoning and writing skills as well as Mathematical concept. Meanwhile, ACT or the American College Test is an achievement test that is administered to assess aptitude skills, reasoning, and verbal abilities of the student before admitting them to college.

In order to pass these exams and probably acquire high scores in their SAT and ACT exams, they must have their own strategies or techniques. They need to have strategies towards easiness of their exam at the same time acquiring better exam results.

How to Get Flying Scores in Your ACT And SAT Exam?

Raising your score with your ACT and Sat exam could be very critical since there are instances that college administrations are making these exams a bit difficult in order to completely and extremely assess the skills and knowledge of the students. Hence, you need to make your own strategy in order to acquire flying scores upon taking any of these exams.

There are three basic strategies that every student must always initiate in order to achieve high scores and show that they really deserve to be admitted in the school you have taken the exam. These strategies include:

Time Management

In order to enhance your own taking skills, you need to be more particular in managing your time. Most of the students as of today who doesn't have any idea on how to manage their time lose huge number of points because they are already running out of time answering items in the test. But this is not the scenario for students who know how to deal with time management since they can be able to divide their time to the number of items they are supposed to answer.

Quick Way of Answering

The second strategy that you need to do in order to acquire flying scores in your ACT and SAT exam would be your quickness in answering all the items in the exam. Quickness in answering all the questions in the exam doesn't necessarily mean that you need to guess every time you don't have any idea about the correct answer. You need to acquire quickness provided that you know how to clearly understand questions covered by the exam.

Efficient Study Habits

Before taking any of the two types of exam make sure that you spare time studying some of their past lessons in order to assure that they are already ready to take the exam. Aiming for a flying score is not an easy goal without even scanning some of your notes. You always need to study hard before taking the exam since this would be an effective key in achieving high score in the exam.

Focusing and working hard is very important if you really wanted to raise higher score with your ACT and SAT exam. If you are responsible and very dedicated towards your goal then you are significantly qualified and deserving to have a flying score in whatever exam college schools and institutions would be administering.

CHAPTER 3

IS ADVANCE PLACEMENT TEST NECESSARY?

Synopsis

Advance placement test is a type of test that is offered in different subject areas. This is one of the best ways that would effectively and immediately let students to jump off to college without experiencing any difficult admission exams anymore. This is also one way of arousing college readiness of every student who intends to pursue their college education. It is combined with different sets of questions that can effectively assess the learning and the knowledge inculcated in the mind of the student from their previous school days.

Most parents and students are not very familiar with this advancement placement test hence they are not aware of this particular type of test would be necessary to be administered in every school. In order to give them a deep glimpse and clear understanding about the essential role of this advance placement in order to be well-educated and be successful in their future endeavor.

Essential Role of Advance Placement Test for Students

☐ It provides students greater chance to adjust to some rigors that may be present in their college days while they are still in their high school pace. This is very essential since it gives students realistic view when they are already sent to college.

☐ Students can acquire college credits by taking this advance placement test from different subjects. Taking this exam is very important since the college credits that are aiming for would be completely given to you depending on your score.

☐ Students who took this advance placement test can greatly impressed college counselors because of your academic record.

☐ Students can enhance their academic skills since this placement test would develop their critical thinking and calculating skills. This will effectively help them in mastering and several skills in order to have a successful college life.

☐ Saving money would also be a reason why advance placement test is necessary since acquainting yourself to be part of this exam, you are assured that you can graduate in college as early as what you expect. Early graduation in college would be a good idea most particularly to students whose financial aid is beyond their reach.

☐ It can always provide you different choices and idea as to what course in college you are going to take. This is because you are given the chance to acquire depth introduction of the subjects that you are going to take in college. Apart from it, raising a high score on this exam would mean that you deserved to take whatever course you wanted to pursue.

☐ It widely open doors or rooms for college opportunities that would make every student acquire easiness in choosing what particular course to take.

Advance placement test is necessary to be administered by different college institutions all over the world. This is because there are so much benefits that this test would be giving not only to the students who are going to pursue their college schooling but most especially to their parents. This is to make sure that both of them would be ready to face all the challenges that they might be encountering on their college life.

CHAPTER 4

YOUR GRADES AND HOW IT STRENGTHENS YOUR APPLICATION

Synopsis

Getting good grades in college must be always one of the top priorities of college students. Your grades play an important role in strengthening your chosen college career. Hence, college students need to work hard in order to achieve good grades not only for the sake of achieving excellent academic awards but most particularly to acquire a successful and fruitful career in the future.

Your grades would be very essential in empowering your own college application. This will serve as your stepping stone in achieving all your dreams in life. Hence, as a student, you need to be responsible in getting good grades in your entire subject. You need to also to be familiar with all the things regarding the importance of your grades and how it effectively helps you in strengthening your career. Knowing these things would effectively motivate and arouse your study interest that is highly needed by every student.

How College Grades Effectively Strengthen Your Chosen Career

College students need to be very particular when it comes to their academic skills since this is the key towards achieving good grades. You also need to be determined and be responsible and hardworking all the time in their studies in order to get higher grades most of the students are dreaming of. College grades can effectively strengthen your career in different ways that could effectively let you acquire successful endeavors in your life.

Great Opportunities

As you acquire good grades on your college years, you are assured that great opportunities await your way. Good grades of students serve as their essential incentive towards landing for a job after graduation. They are given greater chance to land for a permanent job since most companies as of today are very particular with the academic skills of the people they are employing and that is through looking at their grades.

Competitive Edge

Good grades would be very essential to students in order to pursue whatever career they wanted to track. This would strengthen their career effectively that since they have great edge from students who have low grades. Hence, through this good grades good academic credentials would always be presented to companies you wanted to apply for a job.

Strong Respectability

Students who have better grades are highly respected and admired by other students. This would be a significant key that pushes students to exert more time and effort in studying their lessons in school. It is also one way of gaining popularity of your social life since more people particularly students would be admiring your good deeds in school.

Positive Sense of Life

Since more people are already admiring you as an excellent high grade earner student, hence you would be strengthening your application or chosen career since you can already develop more of the positive sense of your life. Once you have positive aspect of your life you are assured that even if you are just a college student more jobs would be waiting for you in the future.

Once a student entered more responsibilities awaits their way before graduating and one of which is to earn better grades. College grades always matters in every aspect of students' life hence every student must work for it.

CHAPTER 5

DISCUSS WITH GUIDANCE COUNSELOR TO CHOOSE YOUR COURSE

Synopsis

Choosing the course that you wanted to take in college might be a bit confusing most especially if you don't have any idea as to what would be the best course that is suitable to your skills and abilities. Although parents may also support and guide their children on the best course for them to pursue, this is still not enough since parents suggestions might be contradicting to what course they wanted to take in college.

This is a common scenario that incoming college students are always experiencing. Thus, in order to lessen their worries and confusion and to give them clear idea with what course to take, students must seek the assistance and guidance of the guidance counselor they intend to enroll. Discussing all these matters to the guidance counselor would be very essential in order to help students to track for the suitable course that would make their life productive and successful in the future.

Role of Guidance Counselor in the Life of the Student

Guidance counselor in every college institution plays an important role not only in helping the school administration to be as progressive and productive as it is but it also plays an essential role in every students college life. Discussing with your school guidance counselor would greatly help the students in different ways and these include:

☐ They greatly help every student to choose the appropriate course that is suited to the level of their knowledge, skills and abilities.

☐ They provide array of knowledge regarding the required skills needed for the different courses that their college institution is catering.

☐ They also give students an advanced idea as to what would be the perfect job opportunities of the entire course offered by the school.

☐ They also spare time giving the student knowledge regarding the financial expenses of the different course and highly emphasized the cost of your chosen course.

☐ They always makes way to open discussion more about related topics more about their career in life as early as possible in order to arouse readiness on their college life.

☐ They discuss confusion problems of the student not only when it comes to the career they wanted to pursue but also with some school administration problems that makes people feel afraid pursuing their college schooling.

Guidance counselor works hand and hand with the school, parents and teachers in order to make every student be well-equipped with the knowledge they need when need in order to deal with their college life. Through the guidance and support that most of the guidance counselor in every school is providing students are assured that they would be tracking the suitable and the best course towards a successful life after graduating in college.

CHAPTER 6

BEGIN RESEARCHING ON COLLEGES AND UNIVERSITIES

Synopsis

As an incoming college student, you need to be responsible in choosing the best course for you to take. Apart from it you need to arouse your awareness in choosing the best college or universities where you should enroll to be equipped with the right knowledge, skills and abilities in order to pursue your chosen career. As early as possible, you need to begin researching on colleges and universities that would enhance and develop your academic and career skills effectively.

Researching is very essential since this would give you advanced information regarding the school or university you wish to enroll. You would be properly guided through these researches not only more about the policies and the rules of the university administration but also more of the financial and career assistance and support that they college or university is providing every student. Knowing the importance of school researches would be very essential towards choosing the best school that would cater to your needs.

Why Start to Make Some Research About College or University

Student must always make sure that they have clear and advanced knowledge on the school they wanted to enroll. Researching in advanced would be very essential to both the parents and the student to prevent wasting of their time, money, and effort due to carelessness in choosing the best college or university that would inculcate the right learning to every student.

Student should always spare time to research to huge number of colleges and universities offering their aspired course. They need not to focus on just one university since not all colleges are providing high quality education as what you expect. Focusing on only one university is not vital since you are disregarding other colleges and universities which have much more to offer that the one you've chose. Researching various names of universities and colleges is very important since it would always provide you great choices of school where you could effectively and conveniently enroll.

Begin to start researching on college and universities are very important since it greatly helps the students in many ways and these include:

- Knowing the exact location of the school or university

- Awareness on the different courses offered by the university

- Being familiar with the college administration school regulation, rules and policies

- Knowing allotted expenses to be spent in the different courses

- Being aware of some people behind the college administration

- Getting acquainted with certain scholarship programs and other financial assistance services that the school is providing

- Being familiar in advanced with the college and university lifestyle

These are just some of important things students might be acquiring if they are going to start researching valuable information to different universities whom you are planning to enroll as early as possible. They are greatly in need to do it in order to make sure that you would not be hurrying selecting the best university that would give you the best college experience and education you are aiming for.

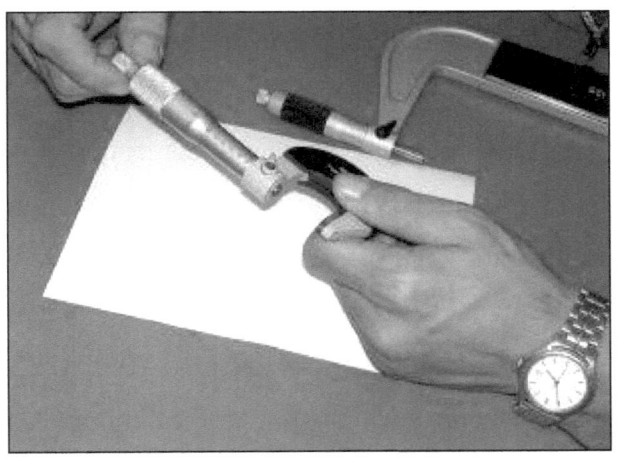

CHAPTER 7

WHAT DOCUMENTS YOU NEED FOR APPLYING TO COLLEGE?

Synopsis

Students cannot pursue college education without complying with the requirements and documents that need to be submitted in order to be admitted to a college or university. School administrations of all universities all over the world are obliging all the students to pass the necessary documents as well as valuable information about your personal identity.

Documents you need for applying college may vary depending on what college or university you wish to enroll. There are huge differences and similarities with some of the requirements schools ask student to submit. This also primarily aims to secure clear records of their students who used to be part of their school.

There are different documents that students must always prepare in order to make sure that they will be admitted to the school where they wanted to enroll. They need to comply and submit complete documents in order to prevent irregularities on the process of submitting all your requirements and documents.

Necessary Documents Required for Applying to College

Students who prepare the needed requirements and documents ahead of time are assured of a simple and systematic college admission processes since they are ready with the complete requirements that the school administration would be asking them. Some of the important requirements that are greatly needed for students to prepare include:

College Application or Admission Forms

This documents are basically been provided by the college or university. It is a form that needs to be filled out by the student for some information about their course and personal identity as well. Student must be always careful in filling out this particular form in by reading all the instructions first before supplying it with the needed information. It is also a must for every student to fill out the form with valuable and reliable information about themselves.

Picture of Different Sizes

Colleges and universities are requiring their student particularly incoming college students to submit their recent photos as part of their identification. You need to prepare several pictures depending on the number of required photos the administration would be asking you to submit.

High School Grades

Incoming college students are obliged to submit their high school grades to the school they intend to enroll. This would serve as a proof that you passed your high school education and you do not have any failing grades in any subject. Your high school grades would also be the basis on determining if you are suitable to the course you wanted to take. It is also one way of getting acquainted with the different scholarship programs of the college and universities provided that your grade is high.

Medical Certificate

Colleges and universities are obliging their students to pass their recent medical certificate since this is one way of assessing the health condition of the student. This is very important since students who have been detected to have illnesses and diseases are given immediate care and treatment.

Good Moral Certificate

This is a certain certificate given to the students who finish their schooling without doing any illegal actions in their previous school attended. This is providing that you are a student of good moral conduct and values.

College Admission Test Results

Since college and universities as of today are administering entrance exams before admitting students in their school, you need to give them the specified score you have acquired upon taking the admission test. This is one of the most important documents that you need to secure and submit to the school that you intend to apply for college.

CHAPTER 8

DEALING WITH COLLEGE APPLICATION PROCESS

Synopsis

As early as possible, students must be equipped with the knowledge as to how they are going to deal with the college application process in order to make sure that they would be completely admitted to the school they wanted to apply. They need to have the skills in advanced to avoid cramming and hurrying as to what school to choose and what course to take.

Students must be well-equipped with essential and effective strategies that could greatly help them in order to have an assurance of acquiring easiness and convenience in dealing with your application processes in college.

Practicing effective strategies would lessen their worries and would completely help them to be free from the unexpected consequences due to late application process you are going to initiate.

Student must always associate different strategies when they aim to be admitted completely and early to the university or college they intend to take their course. They must always follow some of these strategies in order to assure that the college admission processes they are going to encounter would not be as difficult and as harsh as they are expecting.

Strategies on How to Deal With College Admission Processes Easily and Effectively

Careful in Searching

As early as now, make sure that you are already familiar with the best college or university where you intend to enroll. You need to make college and university list that could offer you several choices as to what would be the best school suited for you.

Advanced College or University Visit

After choosing the college or university where to enroll, spare time to visit the school for further information about the requirements, documents, fees, and all other aspects that you need to prepare for. If possible talk to the guidance counselor of the school to seek assistance with the admission process that the school is implementing.

Preparing for All the Documents and Fees

After knowing all the required documents that you need to submit in the school, you need to prepare for it ahead of time. You need to assure that these are complete in order to have easy college admission processes. Apart from the documents, you also need to prepare for the financial expenses depending on the specific course you wanted to take. You may also seek financial assistance to scholarship programs in order to lessen your financial expenses in school.

CHAPTER 9

GETTING FINANCIAL ASSISTANCE
FOR YOU COLLEGE FEES

Synopsis

Many parents are experiencing difficulty today sending their children to college since they can't afford to supply financial expenses of their children. But, they need not to be bothered and stresses when it comes to the financial expenses they are going to spent with the college education of their children since there are financial assistance programs provided by the school and other government institutions that could lessen financial problems of the students. These financial assistance programs are implemented in all college and universities all over the world to cater the needs of deserving students who wanted to pursue their career. This is one way of giving them an opportunity to continue their education journey in college.

Students must be aware as to where they are going to seek for financial assistance that would support their college expenses. They need to seek for this assistance programs as early as possible since there are some programs which are provided for limited number of students only. All they have to do is to prepare and comply with the needed requirements ahead of time in order to have an assurance to be admitted to the financial assistance programs you wish to be part of.

Where to Get Financial Assistance Programs for Your College Fees

You may seek financial assistance programs to school department administration. They are the primary source on how to acquire valuable information regarding financial assistance programs catered by the school. They are responsible for giving students as well as their parents' clear and valuable view as to the different scholarship grants and financial assistance services and programs that the school is implementing.

Apart from it, they are also knowledgeable in supplying students various information regarding scholarship and all other programs which is already outside of their school. This is more of government organizations and associations that are offering financial assistance in their school. More information would be given to students regarding financial assistance programs if they are going to talk personally with the school administration department.

Doing this, students are given the chance to be part of some of these programs. It would also be a great help for them in order to prevent scams that can cost too much of your time, money and effort. They need not to rely more on financial assistance programs online and offered by organizations and people which they are not familiar with, rather choose to talk with the school administration for reliable source of clear and valid information.

CHAPTER 10

PREPARE YOUR FIRST DAY OF COLLEGE

Your first day in college might be a bit fearful and confusing activity since this would be the time that you are going to meet different people from a different environment. In order to overcome your fear, hesitations and confusions, you need to prepare everything for your first day of college. You need to make sure that your mind and body is well-conditioned and ready to face all the things that lie ahead on your fist day of school. Preparing everything would be very essential towards achieving happy and amazing first day college experience.

How to Prepare for Your First Day in College?

There are several that things you need to consider in starting your first day in college right. You need to carry out a certain college plan in order to ensure an amazing and systematic first day in school. Here are some of the important preparations that you need to practice as part of your first day of college preparation:

Know Your Schedule

Knowing your schedule is an essential way on how to start your college day. You need to keep your schedule close to you and if possible familiarize with your schedule before the first day of your school.

Carry Snacks and Foods to Eat

Since it is your first day and you have no idea with the school campus yet, make sure that you have with you foods to eat in order to be prepared in instances that you are already hungry and you are not familiar with the canteen inside the school.

Prepare for Your School Supplies

You need to make sure that you all the things you need in school is already placed in your bag. These include your notebooks, pens, paper and all other important things that is highly needed not only during your first day in college but also in your entire college days.

Arrive Early

Make sure that on the first day of your school, you need to come early in order to acquire time and deal with new friends and adopt as early as possible the new environment you are about to face for a couple of years.

Be Open-Minded

Accept and make sure to spend time to mingle with your friends. You need to get along with them in order to gather new friends that would make your college life happier and more fulfilling.

These are some of the important things that students need to prepare in order to make their first day in college fulfilling and exciting as well as free from fears and hesitations.

Printed by Libri Plureos GmbH in Hamburg, Germany